morning sunshine

a breath of fresh air

Star Boyle

morning sunshine
Copyright © 2021 by Star Boyle

Tellwell Talent
www.tellwell.ca

ISBN
978-0-2288-6678-7 (Paperback)

I'm Star and I will be sharing some insights behind the idea of this journal with you. When you come to this space, I hope you are reminded of each new day having its very own fresh start, similar to you and your goals. The world is yours to design the life you've dreamed of having. I encourage you to create a space where you come to with this journal each day!

The time that I dedicate to myself each and every morning has brought an incredible amount of peace to my mind and body. When I wake up and choose myself over and over again, it serves as a powerful reminder to dream bigger, commit again, and it's a stepping stone for the life I want to have and the person that I want to be. I hope this journal becomes your breath of fresh air every single day.

"A goal that is not in writing is merely a fantasy"
- Darren Hardy

This journal is yours for the next 3 months! I want to walk you through my idea behind each section so that you can make the most out of your time here.

Commitment: We all have 24 hours in a day. What are you choosing to get done - no matter what comes your way. Three things, big or small - let's go win today! Honour your commitments by following through on YOUR word. This is how you build credibility with yourself.

When you give yourself time to think about the goals you want to achieve, in the next 10 years, what comes to mind? What does your family life look like, your career, income, relationships, ect. And when you write each goal down, write them down as if you have already achieved them. Write it. Say it. See it. FEEL it.

This practice alone completely changed the way my brain views life. I had to train my brain for good, instead of lingering in my own self misery. Every single day we have so much to be grateful for. It may feel weird or hard at first, and that's okay. If you can't think of anything, start with simple things such as your body - arms to hug family members, legs to take you around. Think about what's happened in the last 24 hours!

When I think of all the opportunities available to you and me, it's wild to think that there are so many things happening in our lives, and opportunities we haven't even thought of yet! The people you'll meet, the advances in your career, deepening connections with loved ones, creating financial abundance, starting a life with somebody else… The opportunities are endless!

> *"Don't tell me the sky's the limit when*
> *there are footprints on the moon."*
> - Paul Brandt.

I never used to dream or sit and visualize the life I wanted, I didn't know how or even how powerful this practice can be. With this section, I either put on inspiring instrumental music, a podcast or an encouraging Youtube clip and just sit still for as long as the moment allows. There is something about music, or listening to someone speak over my life, that brings the image to reality. My go-to girl is Amanda Frances. When you feel the life or success' you want, you become unstoppable. There are no rules to this journal - these are just some starting points! It is all up to you!

Last but not least, is the affirmation section. This is the area where I will write down whatever I need to hear or feel! "I am good enough", "everything that I desire is available to me". I will often carry these one-liners around with me throughout the day. Feel free to say them as often as you need, repeat the same affirmations, change them up daily, or even write them on sticky notes and place them around your house. Repeating these one-liners can change what you choose to focus on. Choose the good because we all have greatness inside of us, and it's time you start living your life, like your wildest dreams have already come true!

xxx.

Date: ....

What am I committed to make happen today, no matter what.

>

> ⌒ Star Boyle

>

10 big dreams I will accomplish in the next 10 years.

>

>

>

>

>

>

>

>

>

>

10 things that I'm feeling grateful for are…

>

>

>

>

>

>

>

>

>

>

What opportunities lie ahead of me…

Visualize my… (day, success)

Affirmations I need to hear, say, and write down are...

Date: ....

What am I committed to make happen today, no matter what.
>

>

>

10 big dreams I will accomplish in the next 10 years.
>

>

>

>

>

>

>

>

>

>

10 things that I'm feeling grateful for are…
>

>

>

>

>

>

>

>

>

>

What opportunities lie ahead of me…

Visualize my… (day, success)

Affirmations I need to hear, say, and write down are...

Date: ....

What am I committed to make happen today, no matter what.

>

> Star Boyle

>

10 big dreams I will accomplish in the next 10 years.

>

>

>

>

>

>

>

>

>

>

10 things that I'm feeling grateful for are…

>

>

>

>

>

>

>

>

>

>

What opportunities lie ahead of me…

____

____

____

____

____

____

____

Visualize my… (day, success)

____

____

____

____

____

____

____

Affirmations I need to hear, say, and write down are...

____

____

____

____

____

____

____

Date: ………………………………………………………………………………………………………

What am I committed to make happen today, no matter what.

>

>   Star Boyle

>

10 big dreams I will accomplish in the next 10 years.

>

>

>

>

>

>

>

>

>

>

10 things that I'm feeling grateful for are…

>

>

>

>

>

>

>

>

>

>

What opportunities lie ahead of me…

____

____

____

____

____

____

____

____

Visualize my… (day, success)

____

____

____

____

____

____

____

____

Affirmations I need to hear, say, and write down are...

____

____

____

____

____

____

____

Date: ……

What am I committed to make happen today, no matter what.

>

>

>

10 big dreams I will accomplish in the next 10 years.

>

>

>

>

>

>

>

>

>

>

10 things that I'm feeling grateful for are…

>

>

>

>

>

>

>

>

>

>

What opportunities lie ahead of me…

____

____

____

____

____

____

____

Visualize my… (day, success)

____

____

____

____

____

____

____

Affirmations I need to hear, say, and write down are...

____

____

____

____

____

____

____

Date: ....

What am I committed to make happen today, no matter what.

>

>

>

10 big dreams I will accomplish in the next 10 years.

>

>

>

>

>

>

>

>

>

>

10 things that I'm feeling grateful for are…

>

>

>

>

>

>

>

>

>

>

What opportunities lie ahead of me…

____

____

____

____

____

____

____

Visualize my… (day, success)

____

____

____

____

____

____

____

Affirmations I need to hear, say, and write down are...

____

____

____

____

____

____

____

Date: ....

What am I committed to make happen today, no matter what.

\>

\>

\>

10 big dreams I will accomplish in the next 10 years.

\>

\>

\>

\>

\>

\>

\>

\>

\>

\>

10 things that I'm feeling grateful for are…

\>

\>

\>

\>

\>

\>

\>

\>

\>

\>

What opportunities lie ahead of me…

____

____

____

____

____

____

____

Visualize my… (day, success)

____

____

____

____

____

____

____

Affirmations I need to hear, say, and write down are...

____

____

____

____

____

____

____

Date: ....

What am I committed to make happen today, no matter what.

>

>

>

10 big dreams I will accomplish in the next 10 years.

>

>

>

>

>

>

>

>

>

>

10 things that I'm feeling grateful for are…

>

>

>

>

>

>

>

>

>

>

What opportunities lie ahead of me…

Visualize my… (day, success)

Affirmations I need to hear, say, and write down are...

Date: ....

What am I committed to make happen today, no matter what.

>

>

>

10 big dreams I will accomplish in the next 10 years.

>

>

>

>

>

>

>

>

>

>

10 things that I'm feeling grateful for are…

>

>

>

>

>

>

>

>

>

What opportunities lie ahead of me…

____

____

____

____

____

____

____

Visualize my… (day, success)

____

____

____

____

____

____

____

Affirmations I need to hear, say, and write down are...

____

____

____

____

____

____

____

Date: ....

What am I committed to make happen today, no matter what.

>

>

>

10 big dreams I will accomplish in the next 10 years.

>

>

>

>

>

>

>

>

>

>

10 things that I'm feeling grateful for are…

>

>

>

>

>

>

>

>

>

>

What opportunities lie ahead of me…

____

____

____

____

____

____

____

Visualize my… (day, success)

____

____

____

____

____

____

____

Affirmations I need to hear, say, and write down are...

____

____

____

____

____

____

____

Date: ………

What am I committed to make happen today, no matter what.

>

> 🖐 Star Boyle

>

10 big dreams I will accomplish in the next 10 years.

>

>

>

>

>

>

>

>

>

>

10 things that I'm feeling grateful for are…

>

>

>

>

>

>

>

>

>

>

What opportunities lie ahead of me…

____

____

____

____

____

____

Visualize my… (day, success)

____

____

____

____

____

____

____

Affirmations I need to hear, say, and write down are...

____

____

____

____

____

____

____

Date: ....

What am I committed to make happen today, no matter what.

>

> ✎ Star Boyle

>

10 big dreams I will accomplish in the next 10 years.

>

>

>

>

>

>

>

>

>

>

10 things that I'm feeling grateful for are…

>

>

>

>

>

>

>

>

>

>

What opportunities lie ahead of me…

____

____

____

____

____

____

____

Visualize my… (day, success)

____

____

____

____

____

____

____

____

Affirmations I need to hear, say, and write down are...

____

____

____

____

____

____

____

Date: ....

What am I committed to make happen today, no matter what.

>

> Star Boyle

>

10 big dreams I will accomplish in the next 10 years.

>

>

>

>

>

>

>

>

>

>

10 things that I'm feeling grateful for are…

>

>

>

>

>

>

>

>

>

>

What opportunities lie ahead of me…

Visualize my… (day, success)

Affirmations I need to hear, say, and write down are...

Date: ....

What am I committed to make happen today, no matter what.

\>

\> ☞ Star Boyle

\>

10 big dreams I will accomplish in the next 10 years.

\>

\>

\>

\>

\>

\>

\>

\>

\>

\>

10 things that I'm feeling grateful for are…

\>

\>

\>

\>

\>

\>

\>

\>

\>

\>

What opportunities lie ahead of me…

Visualize my… (day, success)

Affirmations I need to hear, say, and write down are...

Date: ....

What am I committed to make happen today, no matter what.

>

> ✐ Star Boyle

>

10 big dreams I will accomplish in the next 10 years.

>

>

>

>

>

>

>

>

>

>

10 things that I'm feeling grateful for are…

>

>

>

>

>

>

>

>

>

>

What opportunities lie ahead of me…

Visualize my… (day, success)

Affirmations I need to hear, say, and write down are...

Date: ....

What am I committed to make happen today, no matter what.

>

>

>

10 big dreams I will accomplish in the next 10 years.

>

>

>

>

>

>

>

>

>

>

10 things that I'm feeling grateful for are…

>

>

>

>

>

>

>

>

>

>

What opportunities lie ahead of me…

____

____

____

____

____

____

____

Visualize my… (day, success)

____

____

____

____

____

____

____

Affirmations I need to hear, say, and write down are...

____

____

____

____

____

____

____

____

Date: ....

What am I committed to make happen today, no matter what.

>

>   Star Boyle

>

10 big dreams I will accomplish in the next 10 years.

>

>

>

>

>

>

>

>

>

>

10 things that I'm feeling grateful for are…

>

>

>

>

>

>

>

>

>

>

What opportunities lie ahead of me…

____

____

____

____

____

____

____

Visualize my… (day, success)

____

____

____

____

____

____

____

Affirmations I need to hear, say, and write down are...

____

____

____

____

____

____

____

Date: ....

What am I committed to make happen today, no matter what.

>

>

>

10 big dreams I will accomplish in the next 10 years.

>

>

>

>

>

>

>

>

>

>

10 things that I'm feeling grateful for are…

>

>

>

>

>

>

>

>

>

>

What opportunities lie ahead of me…

____

____

____

____

____

____

____

Visualize my… (day, success)

____

____

____

____

____

____

____

Affirmations I need to hear, say, and write down are...

____

____

____

____

____

____

____

Date: ....

What am I committed to make happen today, no matter what.

>

>

>

10 big dreams I will accomplish in the next 10 years.

>

>

>

>

>

>

>

>

>

>

10 things that I'm feeling grateful for are…

>

>

>

>

>

>

>

>

>

>

What opportunities lie ahead of me…

____

____

____

____

____

____

____

Visualize my… (day, success)

____

____

____

____

____

____

____

Affirmations I need to hear, say, and write down are...

____

____

____

____

____

____

____

Date: ....

What am I committed to make happen today, no matter what.

>

> ✎ Star Boyle

>

10 big dreams I will accomplish in the next 10 years.

>

>

>

>

>

>

>

>

>

>

10 things that I'm feeling grateful for are…

>

>

>

>

>

>

>

>

>

>

What opportunities lie ahead of me…

____

____

____

____

____

____

____

____

Visualize my… (day, success)

____

____

____

____

____

____

____

____

Affirmations I need to hear, say, and write down are...

____

____

____

____

____

____

____

____

Date: ....

What am I committed to make happen today, no matter what.
>

>

>

10 big dreams I will accomplish in the next 10 years.
>

>

>

>

>

>

>

>

>

>

10 things that I'm feeling grateful for are…
>

>

>

>

>

>

>

>

>

>

What opportunities lie ahead of me…

Visualize my… (day, success)

Affirmations I need to hear, say, and write down are...

Date: ....

What am I committed to make happen today, no matter what.

>

>

>

10 big dreams I will accomplish in the next 10 years.

>

>

>

>

>

>

>

>

>

>

10 things that I'm feeling grateful for are…

>

>

>

>

>

>

>

>

>

>

What opportunities lie ahead of me…

____

____

____

____

____

____

____

Visualize my… (day, success)

____

____

____

____

____

____

____

Affirmations I need to hear, say, and write down are...

____

____

____

____

____

____

____

Date: ....

What am I committed to make happen today, no matter what.

>

>

>

10 big dreams I will accomplish in the next 10 years.

>

>

>

>

>

>

>

>

>

>

10 things that I'm feeling grateful for are…

>

>

>

>

>

>

>

>

>

>

What opportunities lie ahead of me…

Visualize my… (day, success)

Affirmations I need to hear, say, and write down are...

Date: ....

What am I committed to make happen today, no matter what.

>

>   Star Boyle

>

10 big dreams I will accomplish in the next 10 years.

>

>

>

>

>

>

>

>

>

>

10 things that I'm feeling grateful for are…

>

>

>

>

>

>

>

>

>

>

What opportunities lie ahead of me…

Visualize my… (day, success)

Affirmations I need to hear, say, and write down are...

Date: ....

What am I committed to make happen today, no matter what.

>

>   ☁ Star Boyle

>

10 big dreams I will accomplish in the next 10 years.

>

>

>

>

>

>

>

>

>

>

10 things that I'm feeling grateful for are…

>

>

>

>

>

>

>

>

>

>

What opportunities lie ahead of me…

____

____

____

____

____

____

____

Visualize my… (day, success)

____

____

____

____

____

____

____

Affirmations I need to hear, say, and write down are...

____

____

____

____

____

____

____

Date: ....

What am I committed to make happen today, no matter what.

>

>   ☞ Star Boyle

>

10 big dreams I will accomplish in the next 10 years.

>

>

>

>

>

>

>

>

>

>

10 things that I'm feeling grateful for are…

>

>

>

>

>

>

>

>

>

>

What opportunities lie ahead of me…

Visualize my… (day, success)

Affirmations I need to hear, say, and write down are...

Date: ....

What am I committed to make happen today, no matter what.

>

>   Star Boyle

>

10 big dreams I will accomplish in the next 10 years.

>

>

>

>

>

>

>

>

>

>

10 things that I'm feeling grateful for are…

>

>

>

>

>

>

>

>

>

>

What opportunities lie ahead of me…

Visualize my… (day, success)

Affirmations I need to hear, say, and write down are...

Date: ....

What am I committed to make happen today, no matter what.

>

>

>

10 big dreams I will accomplish in the next 10 years.

>

>

>

>

>

>

>

>

>

>

10 things that I'm feeling grateful for are…

>

>

>

>

>

>

>

>

>

>

What opportunities lie ahead of me…

____

____

____

____

____

____

____

Visualize my… (day, success)

____

____

____

____

____

____

Affirmations I need to hear, say, and write down are...

____

____

____

____

____

____

____

Date: ....

What am I committed to make happen today, no matter what.

>

>

>

10 big dreams I will accomplish in the next 10 years.

>

>

>

>

>

>

>

>

>

>

10 things that I'm feeling grateful for are…

>

>

>

>

>

>

>

>

>

>

What opportunities lie ahead of me…

____

____

____

____

____

____

____

Visualize my… (day, success)

____

____

____

____

____

____

____

Affirmations I need to hear, say, and write down are...

____

____

____

____

____

____

____

Date: ....

What am I committed to make happen today, no matter what.

>

>

>

10 big dreams I will accomplish in the next 10 years.

>

>

>

>

>

>

>

>

>

>

10 things that I'm feeling grateful for are…

>

>

>

>

>

>

>

>

>

>

What opportunities lie ahead of me…

Visualize my… (day, success)

Affirmations I need to hear, say, and write down are...

Date: ....

What am I committed to make happen today, no matter what.

>

>

>

10 big dreams I will accomplish in the next 10 years.

>

>

>

>

>

>

>

>

>

>

10 things that I'm feeling grateful for are…

>

>

>

>

>

>

>

>

>

>

What opportunities lie ahead of me…

____

____

____

____

____

____

____

Visualize my… (day, success)

____

____

____

____

____

____

____

Affirmations I need to hear, say, and write down are...

____

____

____

____

____

____

____

Date: ....

What am I committed to make happen today, no matter what.

>

>

>

10 big dreams I will accomplish in the next 10 years.

>

>

>

>

>

>

>

>

>

>

10 things that I'm feeling grateful for are…

>

>

>

>

>

>

>

>

>

>

What opportunities lie ahead of me…

Visualize my… (day, success)

Affirmations I need to hear, say, and write down are...

Date: ....

What am I committed to make happen today, no matter what.

>

>

>

10 big dreams I will accomplish in the next 10 years.

>

>

>

>

>

>

>

>

>

>

10 things that I'm feeling grateful for are…

>

>

>

>

>

>

>

>

>

>

What opportunities lie ahead of me…

____

____

____

____

____

____

____

Visualize my… (day, success)

____

____

____

____

____

____

____

Affirmations I need to hear, say, and write down are...

____

____

____

____

____

____

____

Date: ....

What am I committed to make happen today, no matter what.

>

>

>

10 big dreams I will accomplish in the next 10 years.

>

>

>

>

>

>

>

>

>

>

10 things that I'm feeling grateful for are…

>

>

>

>

>

>

>

>

>

>

What opportunities lie ahead of me…

____

____

____

____

____

____

____

Visualize my… (day, success)

____

____

____

____

____

____

____

Affirmations I need to hear, say, and write down are...

____

____

____

____

____

____

____

Date: ....

What am I committed to make happen today, no matter what.

>

>

>

10 big dreams I will accomplish in the next 10 years.

>

>

>

>

>

>

>

>

>

>

10 things that I'm feeling grateful for are…

>

>

>

>

>

>

>

>

>

>

What opportunities lie ahead of me…

____

____

____

____

____

____

____

Visualize my… (day, success)

____

____

____

____

____

____

____

Affirmations I need to hear, say, and write down are...

____

____

____

____

____

____

____

Date: ....

What am I committed to make happen today, no matter what.

>

>   ✎ Star Boyle

>

10 big dreams I will accomplish in the next 10 years.

>

>

>

>

>

>

>

>

>

>

10 things that I'm feeling grateful for are…

>

>

>

>

>

>

>

>

>

>

What opportunities lie ahead of me…

Visualize my… (day, success)

Affirmations I need to hear, say, and write down are...

Date: ....

What am I committed to make happen today, no matter what.

>

> ☞ Star Boyle

>

10 big dreams I will accomplish in the next 10 years.

>

>

>

>

>

>

>

>

>

>

10 things that I'm feeling grateful for are…

>

>

>

>

>

>

>

>

>

>

What opportunities lie ahead of me…

Visualize my… (day, success)

Affirmations I need to hear, say, and write down are...

Date: ....

What am I committed to make happen today, no matter what.
>

>   ✍ Star Boyle
>

10 big dreams I will accomplish in the next 10 years.
>

>

>

>

>

>

>

>

>

>

10 things that I'm feeling grateful for are…
>

>

>

>

>

>

>

>

>

>

What opportunities lie ahead of me…

Visualize my… (day, success)

Affirmations I need to hear, say, and write down are...

Date: ....

What am I committed to make happen today, no matter what.
>

>

>

10 big dreams I will accomplish in the next 10 years.
>

>

>

>

>

>

>

>

>

>

10 things that I'm feeling grateful for are…
>

>

>

>

>

>

>

>

>

>

What opportunities lie ahead of me…

Visualize my… (day, success)

Affirmations I need to hear, say, and write down are...

Date: ……

What am I committed to make happen today, no matter what.

>

>   ☁ Star Boyle

>

10 big dreams I will accomplish in the next 10 years.

>

>

>

>

>

>

>

>

>

>

10 things that I'm feeling grateful for are…

>

>

>

>

>

>

>

>

>

What opportunities lie ahead of me…

Visualize my… (day, success)

Affirmations I need to hear, say, and write down are...

Date: ....

What am I committed to make happen today, no matter what.

>

>

>

10 big dreams I will accomplish in the next 10 years.

>

>

>

>

>

>

>

>

>

>

10 things that I'm feeling grateful for are…

>

>

>

>

>

>

>

>

>

>

What opportunities lie ahead of me…

____

____

____

____

____

____

____

Visualize my… (day, success)

____

____

____

____

____

____

____

Affirmations I need to hear, say, and write down are...

____

____

____

____

____

____

____

Date: ....

What am I committed to make happen today, no matter what.

\>

\> ✐ Star Boyle

\>

10 big dreams I will accomplish in the next 10 years.

\>

\>

\>

\>

\>

\>

\>

\>

\>

\>

10 things that I'm feeling grateful for are…

\>

\>

\>

\>

\>

\>

\>

\>

\>

\>

What opportunities lie ahead of me…

Visualize my… (day, success)

Affirmations I need to hear, say, and write down are...

Date: ....

What am I committed to make happen today, no matter what.

>

>   Star Boyle

>

10 big dreams I will accomplish in the next 10 years.

>

>

>

>

>

>

>

>

>

>

10 things that I'm feeling grateful for are…

>

>

>

>

>

>

>

>

>

>

What opportunities lie ahead of me…

____

____

____

____

____

____

____

Visualize my… (day, success)

____

____

____

____

____

____

____

Affirmations I need to hear, say, and write down are...

____

____

____

____

____

____

____

Date: ....

What am I committed to make happen today, no matter what.

>

>

>

10 big dreams I will accomplish in the next 10 years.

>

>

>

>

>

>

>

>

>

>

10 things that I'm feeling grateful for are…

>

>

>

>

>

>

>

>

>

>

What opportunities lie ahead of me…

Visualize my… (day, success)

Affirmations I need to hear, say, and write down are...

Date: ....

What am I committed to make happen today, no matter what.

>

>

>

10 big dreams I will accomplish in the next 10 years.

>

>

>

>

>

>

>

>

>

>

10 things that I'm feeling grateful for are…

>

>

>

>

>

>

>

>

>

>

What opportunities lie ahead of me…

Visualize my… (day, success)

Affirmations I need to hear, say, and write down are...

Date: ....

What am I committed to make happen today, no matter what.

>

>   Star Boyle

>

10 big dreams I will accomplish in the next 10 years.

>

>

>

>

>

>

>

>

>

>

10 things that I'm feeling grateful for are…

>

>

>

>

>

>

>

>

>

>

What opportunities lie ahead of me…

Visualize my… (day, success)

Affirmations I need to hear, say, and write down are...

Date: ....

What am I committed to make happen today, no matter what.

>

>

>

10 big dreams I will accomplish in the next 10 years.

>

>

>

>

>

>

>

>

>

>

10 things that I'm feeling grateful for are…

>

>

>

>

>

>

>

>

>

>

What opportunities lie ahead of me…

____

____

____

____

____

____

____

Visualize my… (day, success)

____

____

____

____

____

____

____

Affirmations I need to hear, say, and write down are...

____

____

____

____

____

____

____

Date: ………

What am I committed to make happen today, no matter what.

>

>   Star Boyle

>

10 big dreams I will accomplish in the next 10 years.

>

>

>

>

>

>

>

>

>

>

10 things that I'm feeling grateful for are…

>

>

>

>

>

>

>

>

>

>

What opportunities lie ahead of me…

Visualize my… (day, success)

Affirmations I need to hear, say, and write down are...

Date: ....

What am I committed to make happen today, no matter what.

>

>

>

10 big dreams I will accomplish in the next 10 years.

>

>

>

>

>

>

>

>

>

>

10 things that I'm feeling grateful for are…

>

>

>

>

>

>

>

>

>

>

What opportunities lie ahead of me…

____

____

____

____

____

____

____

Visualize my… (day, success)

____

____

____

____

____

____

____

Affirmations I need to hear, say, and write down are...

____

____

____

____

____

____

____

Date: ....

What am I committed to make happen today, no matter what.

>

>

>

10 big dreams I will accomplish in the next 10 years.

>

>

>

>

>

>

>

>

>

>

10 things that I'm feeling grateful for are…

>

>

>

>

>

>

>

>

>

>

What opportunities lie ahead of me…

____

____

____

____

____

____

____

Visualize my… (day, success)

____

____

____

____

____

____

____

Affirmations I need to hear, say, and write down are...

____

____

____

____

____

____

____

Date: ....

What am I committed to make happen today, no matter what.

>

>   Star Boyle

>

10 big dreams I will accomplish in the next 10 years.

>

>

>

>

>

>

>

>

>

>

10 things that I'm feeling grateful for are…

>

>

>

>

>

>

>

>

>

>

What opportunities lie ahead of me…

Visualize my… (day, success)

Affirmations I need to hear, say, and write down are...

Date: ....

What am I committed to make happen today, no matter what.

>

>   Star Boyle

>

10 big dreams I will accomplish in the next 10 years.

>

>

>

>

>

>

>

>

>

>

10 things that I'm feeling grateful for are…

>

>

>

>

>

>

>

>

>

What opportunities lie ahead of me…

____

____

____

____

____

____

____

Visualize my… (day, success)

____

____

____

____

____

____

____

Affirmations I need to hear, say, and write down are…

____

____

____

____

____

____

____

Date: ………………………………………………………………………………………………

What am I committed to make happen today, no matter what.

>

>

>

10 big dreams I will accomplish in the next 10 years.

>

>

>

>

>

>

>

>

>

>

10 things that I'm feeling grateful for are…

>

>

>

>

>

>

>

>

>

>

What opportunities lie ahead of me…

Visualize my… (day, success)

Affirmations I need to hear, say, and write down are...

Date: ....

What am I committed to make happen today, no matter what.

>

>   ✎ Star Boyle

>

10 big dreams I will accomplish in the next 10 years.

>

>

>

>

>

>

>

>

>

>

10 things that I'm feeling grateful for are…

>

>

>

>

>

>

>

>

>

What opportunities lie ahead of me…

Visualize my… (day, success)

Affirmations I need to hear, say, and write down are...

Date: ....

What am I committed to make happen today, no matter what.

>

>   Star Boyle

>

10 big dreams I will accomplish in the next 10 years.

>

>

>

>

>

>

>

>

>

>

10 things that I'm feeling grateful for are…

>

>

>

>

>

>

>

>

>

>

What opportunities lie ahead of me…

____

____

____

____

____

____

____

Visualize my… (day, success)

____

____

____

____

____

____

____

Affirmations I need to hear, say, and write down are...

____

____

____

____

____

____

____

Date: ....

What am I committed to make happen today, no matter what.

>

>

>

10 big dreams I will accomplish in the next 10 years.

>

>

>

>

>

>

>

>

>

>

10 things that I'm feeling grateful for are…

>

>

>

>

>

>

>

>

>

>

What opportunities lie ahead of me…

Visualize my… (day, success)

Affirmations I need to hear, say, and write down are...

Date: ....

What am I committed to make happen today, no matter what.

>

>

>

10 big dreams I will accomplish in the next 10 years.

>

>

>

>

>

>

>

>

>

>

10 things that I'm feeling grateful for are…

>

>

>

>

>

>

>

>

>

>

What opportunities lie ahead of me…

\

Visualize my… (day, success)

\

Affirmations I need to hear, say, and write down are...

Date: ....

What am I committed to make happen today, no matter what.

>

>

>

10 big dreams I will accomplish in the next 10 years.

>

>

>

>

>

>

>

>

>

>

10 things that I'm feeling grateful for are…

>

>

>

>

>

>

>

>

>

>

What opportunities lie ahead of me…

____

____

____

____

____

____

____

Visualize my… (day, success)

____

____

____

____

____

____

____

Affirmations I need to hear, say, and write down are...

____

____

____

____

____

____

____

Date: ....

What am I committed to make happen today, no matter what.

>

>

>

10 big dreams I will accomplish in the next 10 years.

>

>

>

>

>

>

>

>

>

>

10 things that I'm feeling grateful for are…

>

>

>

>

>

>

>

>

>

>

What opportunities lie ahead of me…

____

____

____

____

____

____

____

Visualize my… (day, success)

____

____

____

____

____

____

____

Affirmations I need to hear, say, and write down are...

____

____

____

____

____

____

____

Date: ....

What am I committed to make happen today, no matter what.

>

>

>

10 big dreams I will accomplish in the next 10 years.

>

>

>

>

>

>

>

>

>

>

10 things that I'm feeling grateful for are…

>

>

>

>

>

>

>

>

>

>

What opportunities lie ahead of me…

Visualize my… (day, success)

Affirmations I need to hear, say, and write down are...

Date: ....

What am I committed to make happen today, no matter what.

>

>

>

10 big dreams I will accomplish in the next 10 years.

>

>

>

>

>

>

>

>

>

>

10 things that I'm feeling grateful for are…

>

>

>

>

>

>

>

>

>

>

What opportunities lie ahead of me…

Visualize my… (day, success)

Affirmations I need to hear, say, and write down are...

Date: ………

What am I committed to make happen today, no matter what.
>
>
>

10 big dreams I will accomplish in the next 10 years.
>
>
>
>
>
>
>
>
>
>

10 things that I'm feeling grateful for are…
>
>
>
>
>
>
>
>
>
>

What opportunities lie ahead of me…

____

____

____

____

____

____

Visualize my… (day, success)

____

____

____

____

____

____

Affirmations I need to hear, say, and write down are...

____

____

____

____

____

____

____

Date: ....

What am I committed to make happen today, no matter what.

>

> 8 ✎ Star Boyle

>

10 big dreams I will accomplish in the next 10 years.

>

>

>

>

>

>

>

>

>

>

10 things that I'm feeling grateful for are…

>

>

>

>

>

>

>

>

>

>

What opportunities lie ahead of me…

____

____

____

____

____

____

____

Visualize my… (day, success)

____

____

____

____

____

____

____

____

Affirmations I need to hear, say, and write down are...

____

____

____

____

____

____

____

Date: ....

What am I committed to make happen today, no matter what.

>

>

>

10 big dreams I will accomplish in the next 10 years.

>

>

>

>

>

>

>

>

>

>

10 things that I'm feeling grateful for are…

>

>

>

>

>

>

>

>

>

>

What opportunities lie ahead of me…

Visualize my… (day, success)

Affirmations I need to hear, say, and write down are...

Date: ....

What am I committed to make happen today, no matter what.

>

>

>

10 big dreams I will accomplish in the next 10 years.

>

>

>

>

>

>

>

>

>

>

10 things that I'm feeling grateful for are…

>

>

>

>

>

>

>

>

>

>

What opportunities lie ahead of me…

____

____

____

____

____

____

____

Visualize my… (day, success)

____

____

____

____

____

____

____

Affirmations I need to hear, say, and write down are...

____

____

____

____

____

____

____

Date: ....

What am I committed to make happen today, no matter what.

>

>   🖋 Star Boyle

>

10 big dreams I will accomplish in the next 10 years.

>

>

>

>

>

>

>

>

>

>

10 things that I'm feeling grateful for are…

>

>

>

>

>

>

>

>

>

>

What opportunities lie ahead of me…

Visualize my… (day, success)

Affirmations I need to hear, say, and write down are...

Date: ....

What am I committed to make happen today, no matter what.

>

>

>

10 big dreams I will accomplish in the next 10 years.

>

>

>

>

>

>

>

>

>

>

10 things that I'm feeling grateful for are…

>

>

>

>

>

>

>

>

>

>

What opportunities lie ahead of me…

____

____

____

____

____

____

____

Visualize my… (day, success)

____

____

____

____

____

____

____

Affirmations I need to hear, say, and write down are...

____

____

____

____

____

____

____

Date: ………

What am I committed to make happen today, no matter what.

>

>   ◠ Star Boyle

>

10 big dreams I will accomplish in the next 10 years.

>

>

>

>

>

>

>

>

>

>

10 things that I'm feeling grateful for are…

>

>

>

>

>

>

>

>

>

>

What opportunities lie ahead of me…

____

____

____

____

____

____

____

Visualize my… (day, success)

____

____

____

____

____

____

Affirmations I need to hear, say, and write down are...

____

____

____

____

____

____

____

Date: ....

What am I committed to make happen today, no matter what.

>

>

>

10 big dreams I will accomplish in the next 10 years.

>

>

>

>

>

>

>

>

>

>

10 things that I'm feeling grateful for are…

>

>

>

>

>

>

>

>

>

>

What opportunities lie ahead of me…

____

____

____

____

____

____

____

Visualize my… (day, success)

____

____

____

____

____

____

____

Affirmations I need to hear, say, and write down are...

____

____

____

____

____

____

____

Date: ....

What am I committed to make happen today, no matter what.
>

>

>

10 big dreams I will accomplish in the next 10 years.
>

>

>

>

>

>

>

>

>

>

10 things that I'm feeling grateful for are…
>

>

>

>

>

>

>

>

>

>

What opportunities lie ahead of me…

____

____

____

____

____

____

Visualize my… (day, success)

____

____

____

____

____

____

Affirmations I need to hear, say, and write down are...

____

____

____

____

____

____

Date: ....

What am I committed to make happen today, no matter what.

>

>

>

10 big dreams I will accomplish in the next 10 years.

>

>

>

>

>

>

>

>

>

>

10 things that I'm feeling grateful for are…

>

>

>

>

>

>

>

>

>

>

What opportunities lie ahead of me…

____

____

____

____

____

____

____

Visualize my… (day, success)

____

____

____

____

____

____

____

Affirmations I need to hear, say, and write down are...

____

____

____

____

____

____

____

Date: ………

What am I committed to make happen today, no matter what.

>

>

>

10 big dreams I will accomplish in the next 10 years.

>

>

>

>

>

>

>

>

>

>

10 things that I'm feeling grateful for are…

>

>

>

>

>

>

>

>

>

>

What opportunities lie ahead of me…

Visualize my… (day, success)

Affirmations I need to hear, say, and write down are...

Date: ....

What am I committed to make happen today, no matter what.

\>

\>

\>

10 big dreams I will accomplish in the next 10 years.

\>

\>

\>

\>

\>

\>

\>

\>

\>

\>

10 things that I'm feeling grateful for are…

\>

\>

\>

\>

\>

\>

\>

\>

\>

\>

What opportunities lie ahead of me…

Visualize my… (day, success)

Affirmations I need to hear, say, and write down are...

Date: ....

What am I committed to make happen today, no matter what.

>

>

>

10 big dreams I will accomplish in the next 10 years.

>

>

>

>

>

>

>

>

>

>

10 things that I'm feeling grateful for are…

>

>

>

>

>

>

>

>

>

>

What opportunities lie ahead of me…

____

____

____

____

____

Visualize my… (day, success)

____

____

____

____

____

Affirmations I need to hear, say, and write down are…

____

____

____

____

____

____

Date: ....

What am I committed to make happen today, no matter what.

>

>

>

10 big dreams I will accomplish in the next 10 years.

>

>

>

>

>

>

>

>

>

>

10 things that I'm feeling grateful for are…

>

>

>

>

>

>

>

>

>

>

What opportunities lie ahead of me…

Visualize my… (day, success)

Affirmations I need to hear, say, and write down are...

Date: ....

What am I committed to make happen today, no matter what.

\>

\> 4 Star Boyle

\>

10 big dreams I will accomplish in the next 10 years.

\>

\>

\>

\>

\>

\>

\>

\>

\>

\>

10 things that I'm feeling grateful for are…

\>

\>

\>

\>

\>

\>

\>

\>

\>

\>

What opportunities lie ahead of me…

Visualize my… (day, success)

Affirmations I need to hear, say, and write down are...

Date: ....

What am I committed to make happen today, no matter what.

>

> 6 ☞ Star Boyle

>

10 big dreams I will accomplish in the next 10 years.

>

>

>

>

>

>

>

>

>

>

10 things that I'm feeling grateful for are…

>

>

>

>

>

>

>

>

>

>

What opportunities lie ahead of me…

Visualize my… (day, success)

Affirmations I need to hear, say, and write down are...

Date: ....

What am I committed to make happen today, no matter what.

>

>

>

10 big dreams I will accomplish in the next 10 years.

>

>

>

>

>

>

>

>

>

>

10 things that I'm feeling grateful for are…

>

>

>

>

>

>

>

>

>

>

What opportunities lie ahead of me…

____

____

____

____

____

____

____

Visualize my… (day, success)

____

____

____

____

____

____

____

Affirmations I need to hear, say, and write down are...

____

____

____

____

____

____

____

Date: ....

What am I committed to make happen today, no matter what.

>

>

>

10 big dreams I will accomplish in the next 10 years.

>

>

>

>

>

>

>

>

>

>

10 things that I'm feeling grateful for are…

>

>

>

>

>

>

>

>

>

>

What opportunities lie ahead of me…

____

____

____

____

____

____

____

Visualize my… (day, success)

____

____

____

____

____

____

____

Affirmations I need to hear, say, and write down are...

____

____

____

____

____

____

____

Date: ....

What am I committed to make happen today, no matter what.
>
>
>

10 big dreams I will accomplish in the next 10 years.
>
>
>
>
>
>
>
>
>
>

10 things that I'm feeling grateful for are…
>
>
>
>
>
>
>
>
>
>

What opportunities lie ahead of me…

____

____

____

____

____

____

____

Visualize my… (day, success)

____

____

____

____

____

____

____

Affirmations I need to hear, say, and write down are...

____

____

____

____

____

____

____

Date: ....

What am I committed to make happen today, no matter what.

>

> 6 ℯ Star Boyle

>

10 big dreams I will accomplish in the next 10 years.

>

>

>

>

>

>

>

>

>

>

10 things that I'm feeling grateful for are…

>

>

>

>

>

>

>

>

>

What opportunities lie ahead of me…

Visualize my… (day, success)

Affirmations I need to hear, say, and write down are...

Date: ....

What am I committed to make happen today, no matter what.

>

>

>

10 big dreams I will accomplish in the next 10 years.

>

>

>

>

>

>

>

>

>

>

10 things that I'm feeling grateful for are…

>

>

>

>

>

>

>

>

>

>

What opportunities lie ahead of me…

____

____

____

____

____

____

____

Visualize my… (day, success)

____

____

____

____

____

____

____

Affirmations I need to hear, say, and write down are...

____

____

____

____

____

____

____

Date: ……

What am I committed to make happen today, no matter what.

>

> 8

>

10 big dreams I will accomplish in the next 10 years.

>

>

>

>

>

>

>

>

>

>

10 things that I'm feeling grateful for are…

>

>

>

>

>

>

>

>

>

>

What opportunities lie ahead of me…

Visualize my… (day, success)

Affirmations I need to hear, say, and write down are...

Date: ....

What am I committed to make happen today, no matter what.
>

>

>

10 big dreams I will accomplish in the next 10 years.
>

>

>

>

>

>

>

>

>

>

10 things that I'm feeling grateful for are…
>

>

>

>

>

>

>

>

>

>

What opportunities lie ahead of me…

Visualize my… (day, success)

Affirmations I need to hear, say, and write down are...

Date: ....

What am I committed to make happen today, no matter what.

>

> 2

>

10 big dreams I will accomplish in the next 10 years.

>

>

>

>

>

>

>

>

>

>

10 things that I'm feeling grateful for are…

>

>

>

>

>

>

>

>

>

>

What opportunities lie ahead of me…

____

____

____

____

____

____

____

Visualize my… (day, success)

____

____

____

____

____

____

____

Affirmations I need to hear, say, and write down are...

____

____

____

____

____

____

____

Date: ....

What am I committed to make happen today, no matter what.

>

> 4 🐘 Star Boyle

>

10 big dreams I will accomplish in the next 10 years.

>

>

>

>

>

>

>

>

>

>

10 things that I'm feeling grateful for are...

>

>

>

>

>

>

>

>

>

>

What opportunities lie ahead of me…

Visualize my… (day, success)

Affirmations I need to hear, say, and write down are...

What am I committed to make happen today, no matter what.

>

>

>

10 big dreams I will accomplish in the next 10 years.

>

>

>

>

>

>

>

>

>

>

10 things that I'm feeling grateful for are…

>

>

>

>

>

>

>

>

>

>

What opportunities lie ahead of me…

Visualize my… (day, success)

Affirmations I need to hear, say, and write down are...

Date: ....

What am I committed to make happen today, no matter what.

>

> 8 ⌐ Star Boyle

>

10 big dreams I will accomplish in the next 10 years.

>

>

>

>

>

>

>

>

>

>

10 things that I'm feeling grateful for are…

>

>

>

>

>

>

>

>

>

>

What opportunities lie ahead of me…

____

____

____

____

____

____

____

Visualize my… (day, success)

____

____

____

____

____

____

____

Affirmations I need to hear, say, and write down are...

____

____

____

____

____

____

____

Date: ....

What am I committed to make happen today, no matter what.

>

>

>

10 big dreams I will accomplish in the next 10 years.

>

>

>

>

>

>

>

>

>

>

10 things that I'm feeling grateful for are…

>

>

>

>

>

>

>

>

>

>

What opportunities lie ahead of me…

____

____

____

____

____

____

____

Visualize my… (day, success)

____

____

____

____

____

____

Affirmations I need to hear, say, and write down are...

____

____

____

____

____

____

____

Date: ....

What am I committed to make happen today, no matter what.

>

>

>

10 big dreams I will accomplish in the next 10 years.

>

>

>

>

>

>

>

>

>

>

10 things that I'm feeling grateful for are…

>

>

>

>

>

>

>

>

>

>

What opportunities lie ahead of me…

Visualize my… (day, success)

Affirmations I need to hear, say, and write down are...